Messages

from the mystical cards

Gali Lucy

Card design: Yair Wiener

The information contained in this book is in no shape or form a diagnosis, prescription or treatment of any health disorder whatsoever. This information simply presents a suggestion or an opinion of the author and should not replace consultation with a competent healthcare professional. In a case of any medical, mental or psychological problem one must consult a proper health care provider. The author and the publisher are in no way liable for any misuse of the material.

Receiving Messages:

Option A – Choose a number:

1. Think of one question and a number between 1-52.

2. Open the book, on the page corresponding to the message number and read your message.

3. If you wish to continue receiving messages for the same question or a new question, repeat step 1 above, as often as you like.

4. You may also give messages to others, the person asking the question chooses a number between 1-52, and the other reads the message number that matches the page number that they chose. You may repeat this as many times as you would like.

Option B – Choose randomly:

1. Think of one question, open the book on a random page, and read the message.

2. If you would like to continue receiving messages for the same or a new question, repeat step 1, as often as you like.

3. You may give messages to others as well, request the person asking the question to think of a question and randomly open the book for him and read the message.

Divine Message 1

All of you shall care for one another and be as one and I shall gather you from the four corners of the world. I shall uplift your souls from the gutters, to lead you from despair and doom, with the ancient knowledge to 'Tikkun Olam', repairing the world.

Righteousness and purity shall cleanse your thirsty souls, to prepare you for the future, teach you the secrets and unite your souls. In the distant future, I shall wash your faces in turbulent oceans, earthquakes, and signs.

This book is for the generations, contains my words. There is no anger, fury, or punishment - all of me is love.

I prayed to God:
"Let me have everything so that I may enjoy life".

& God replied:
"I gave you life - so that you may enjoy everything".

This message was received from The Creation Entities...

Divine Message 2

Dearly beloved,

who are asking for assistance and guidance in your lives, so you may understand where you should turn to next.

Go to the wise and silent person,

who does not ask for alms or provides you with talismans, who does not walk wearing fine clothes or spends his time in temples and luxurious buildings.

You will reach that person by word of mouth.
Be wise, go to the modest, quiet, and humble ones.

The words of wisdom of heaven are spoken quietly with humor and a smile, not with shouting, threats and intimidation.

Not by might nor by power, but by spirit,
I am the LORD.

This message was received from The Creation Entities...

This book was written using male pronouns, yet it is intended to apply to both genders. I would like to thank all those who purchased, received, or borrowed this book. Nothing is coincidental! This book was meant to fall into your hands.

Do not believe this book, yet create your own truth. There will never be one truth, in order to provide you the freedom to choose, that's why God cannot be one.

All that is required of you, the reader, is curiosity, flexible thinking, a willingness to accept new ideas with an open mind and a healthy sense of humor.

I gathered all of the knowledge, insights, and messages that my soul has collected in its thousands of incarnations. This book was dictated to me at night through channeling with *The Creation's Entities*, first it was directly typed into the computer in Hebrew and then I translated it to English.

Before we begin, here are few basic insights:

There never was and never will be a single truth, because it denies the right to choose. If there was only one truth - you would have been prevented from thinking otherwise.

Two connected rules: freedom of choice and everything goes back to the sender (Karma).

You cannot die.
You are made of spirit which cannot be extinguished.
You're all eternal souls.

God can never be ONE entity.
The universe always allows a free choice between at least two options, that's why God is not one entity but multiple entities which constantly duplicate themselves. It is important that you will have your own personal opinion and way of thinking, open your mind and never blindly follow other people's ideas.

Your aim is to recreate endlessly.
You are originally balls of light, that were lent a soul, temporary guests inside human visual forms across the universe, in order to testify the nature of:
1. Who you are as a spirit.
2. The nature of *The Creation* or God's spirit.

No material will make a soul happy for long.
Nothing was nor will be yours forever other than your free will. Even your soul is not yours! It belongs to *The Creation*!

Abundance confines - scarcity motivates.
The number of souls in the universe is fixed. Every soul that enters - requires another soul to go out, every birth - requires the death of another.

1

Wealthiness

Compensation and reward
come back to life after a long
period of being stranded.
Wealthiness is expected from
thoughtful planning and
investing with caution and
patience, you should check and
not rush to make decisions.
Be grateful for what you have.
Wise and respectful
communication will yield results.
Forgive and learn to come to
terms with your past,
difficulty will disappear
and plenty will come in,
new doors will open to you.

Mystical Cards

··•• Gali Lucy ••··

2

Harmony

This is a new beginning for you,
a change that will lead
to new connections.
Learn to live in **harmony**,
respect the other
without stubbornness and
vulnerability.
Whatever you do,
take responsibility
for your actions,
only you can change
your destiny.

Mystical Cards

• • •   Gali Lucy   • • •

3 Forgiveness

Forgiveness is needed now,
clear your anger and
make peace with a person in your
life, this process
will bring you a sense of
tranquility and understanding
that everything is for your own
benefit. Re-evaluate what you
have been given. Take care of
yourself. Connect with spirituality,
nature, music and other pleasures.
Learn new areas of interest that
will bring you new friendships,
knowledge, career,
abundance and success.

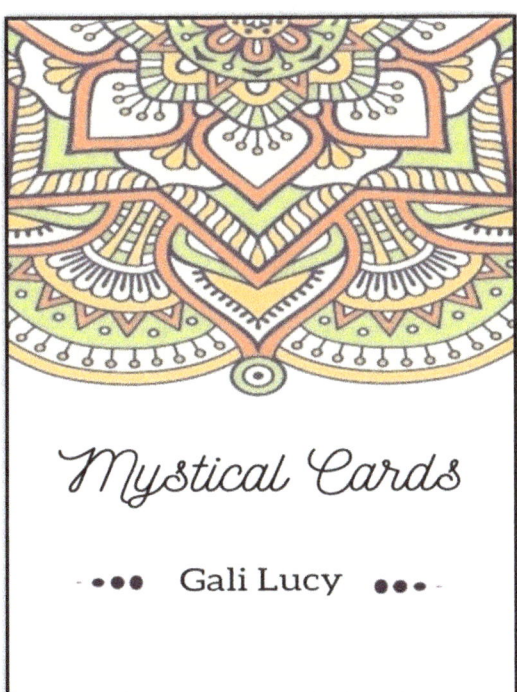

Mystical Cards

··•• Gali Lucy ••··

4

Recompensation

Tensions and disappointment keep you from seeing the situation correctly.
What you do will yield **recompensation**, satisfaction, happiness, success and life experience. Do not rush, try to trust. The Creation will give you freedom of choice and guide you to your destination. Words have the power to heal or crush, everything comes back to your life. You are not obligated to love, but only to respect.

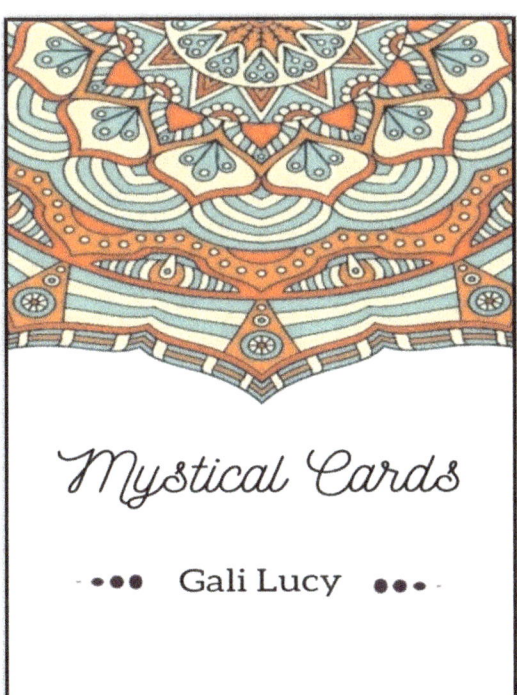

Mystical Cards

• • • Gali Lucy • • •

5

Compromise

You are at a crossroads,
there is a lack of energy
and inner peace to
concentrate. Stubbornness,
criticism and quick decisions
will boost the ego and cause
frustration. The wisdom
is in the silence and
humbleness. Prefer
compromise over war,
act wisely. Relief is expected soon,
difficulty will end
if you respect and are
political. Don't be afraid,
you are guarded and protected.

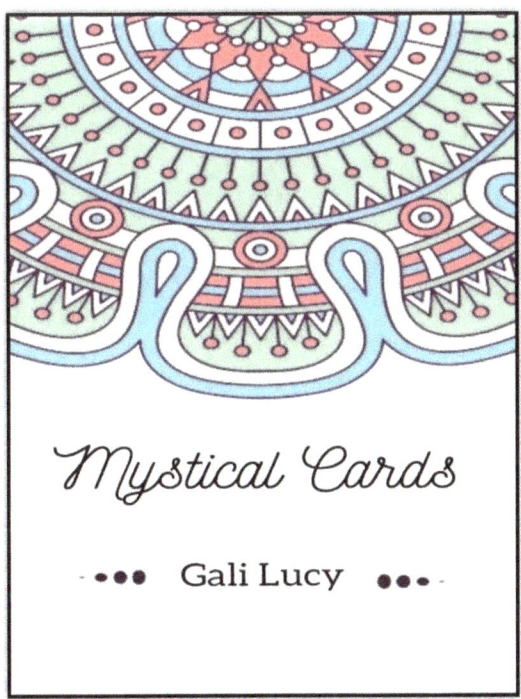

Mystical Cards

••• Gali Lucy •••

6

Decision

You face an important **decision**,
a sense of frustration
and fear of change are blocking
you from seeing accurately.
Apply wisdom over war,
disagreements will be settled
soon. Perseverance and
compromise will produce
results, learn to relax and
pamper your body.
Understand your lesson
and fix your Karma.
Every moment is a new beginning;
decisions are made in your favor.

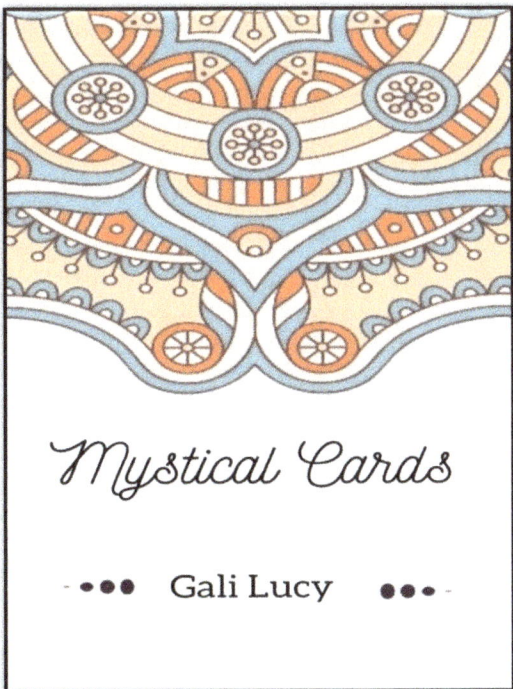

Mystical Cards

· ●●● Gali Lucy ●●● ·

7

Leave

In order to live, you must **leave** and change your thinking patterns regarding your relationships or partnerships.
Release others with love.
Don't be afraid of changes, all is for the best. Encouraging messages are sent to you. You are heading for a new chapter that will bring you happiness, pleasure and health.
Smile over the past and enjoy the present. New social network connections will bring you what you were looking for.

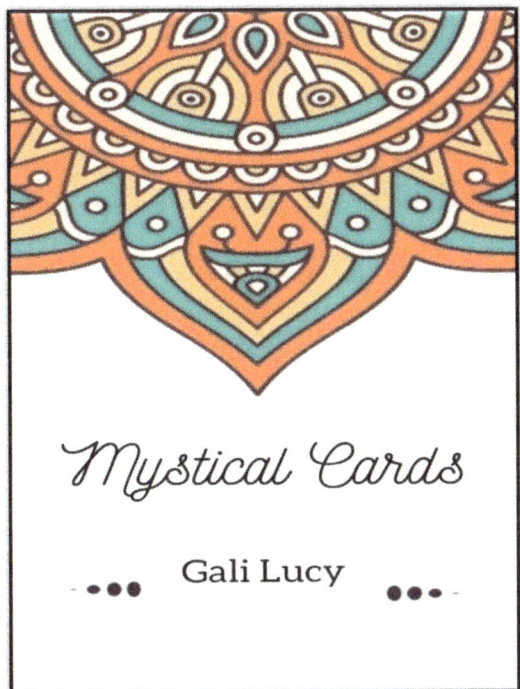

Mystical Cards

Gali Lucy

8

Materialism

There is a great deal of
attention to power and
finance, lack of listening and
patience. Abundant
materialism inhibits progress.
Wealth is not a guarantee
of happiness, listen to your
dreams and criticism from others.
Be grateful for what
you have and don't take it for
granted, as it might disappear
in a second. Try to understand
your purpose in life.
Respect others, as all you do
comes back to you.

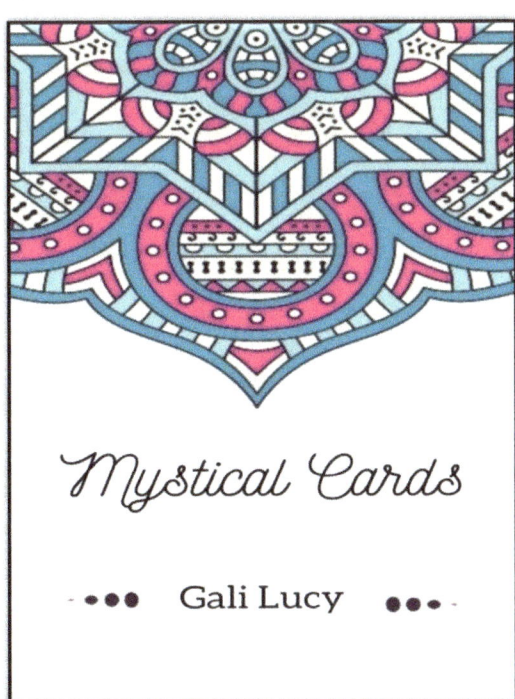

Mystical Cards

- •••   Gali Lucy   ••• -

9

Emotion

There is a struggle between emotion and intellect in life's decisions. You have ancient insights and wisdom, but also frustration, stubbornness and distrust. It is necessary to forgive and act patiently. Express **emotions** to reach closure and to be healthy. You are heading for a good time of study, creativity, meetings and conversations. Re-compensation and abundance will come back to your life.

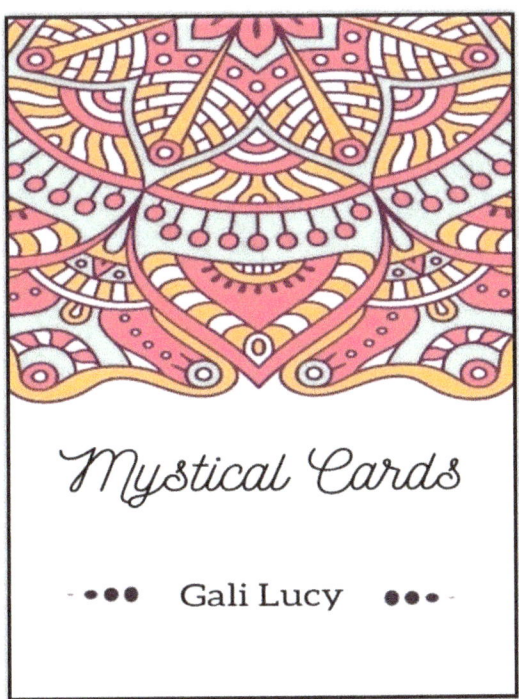

Mystical Cards

••• Gali Lucy •••

10

Desire

There is a **desire** and
motivation which are
fast-reaching to your goals.
Learn to let go with love,
struggles are meant to
make you stronger.
Everything which is stuck
will move in your favor.
You will discover in yourself
new capabilities which you will
also provide to others.
Constant perseverance and
patience are required.
A new creation will be written
by you. Believe that
everything is for the best.

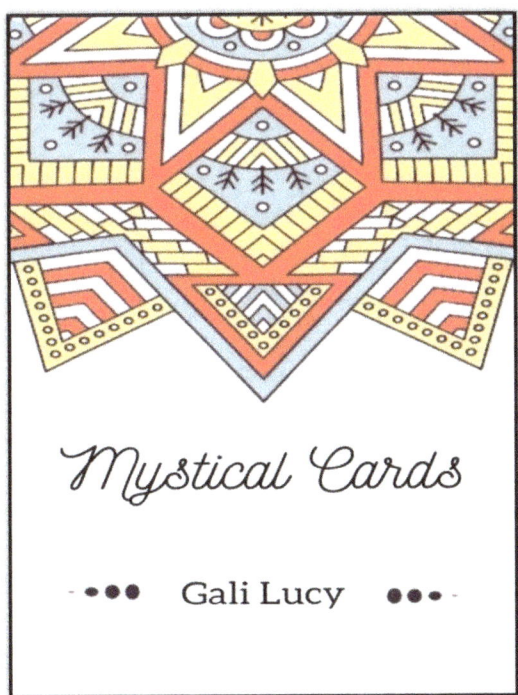

Mystical Cards

••• Gali Lucy •••

11

Success

Positive thinking and
collaborations will bring
you **success** soon.
Judgement and criticism
prevent you from opening
up to new friendships
worldwide. Understand life
as a closure and not as
a mistake. Don't get angry
and learn to forgive.
Happiness is hidden in
the little joys, opportunities
are opening for you,
learn to pick
them up on time.

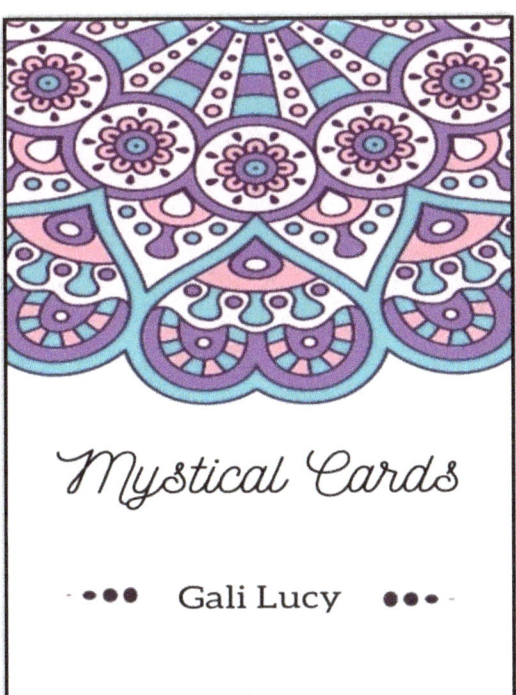

Mystical Cards

••• Gali Lucy •••

12

Awareness

You have a high **awareness**
to guide and direct other
through intuition, ancient
knowledge, experience
and wisdom. An outdated
world view produces
ignorance. Create and don't
copy. You were made to
recreate for the benefit of
humanity. You learn who
you are - through who you
aren't. Every thought or
action comes back to you and
creates the reality of your life.
Happiness and abundance are
coming back to you.

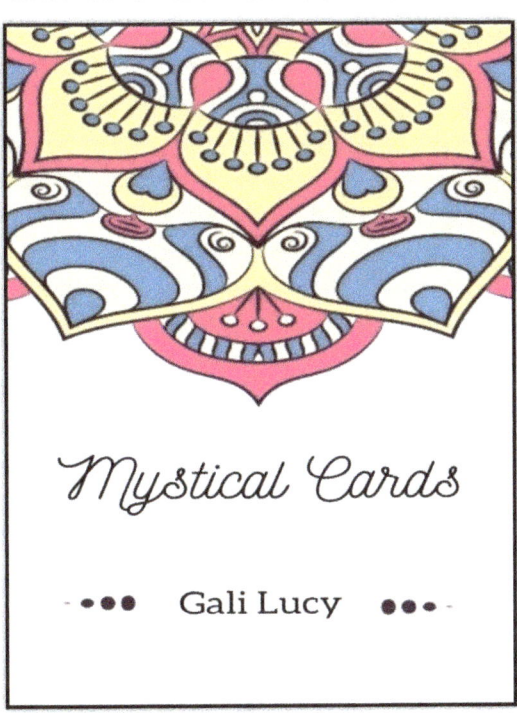

Mystical Cards

- ●●● Gali Lucy ●●● -

13

Change

There is a sense of
insecurity, frustration,
anger, and being blocked.
Change is needed.
Old templates which
completed their job
will vanish if you learn to
forgive and not live the past.
Wisdom will bring you insight.
Do not let others control
you, enjoy every moment
as if it were the last.
Remember; abundance
fixates, and deficiency
drives you.

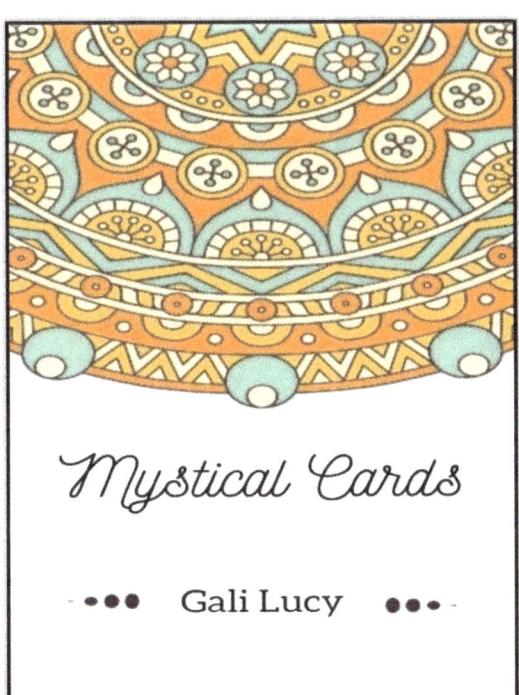

Mystical Cards

••• Gali Lucy •••

14

Acceptance

Stability in life will come
through **acceptance**.
Wise decisions will lead to success,
achievement,
friendships, abundance, and
peace. Learn how to bridge
the gap and balance
between spirit and material,
use humor and optimism. High
expectations and stubbornness
will lead to disappointment,
vulnerability, and frustration.
Allow freedom of choice to all.
Something from the past
is about to end, good
surprises are coming.

Mystical Cards

••• Gali Lucy •••

15

Release

There is a sense of
breakdown, loss, ending,
or **release** from people
who have completed
their roles in your life.
This chaos is necessary
to recreate. You need to
listen with patience,
move away from
ego and stubbornness.
Creation will help and
connect you with people
who will bring you
abundance and
re-appreciation.

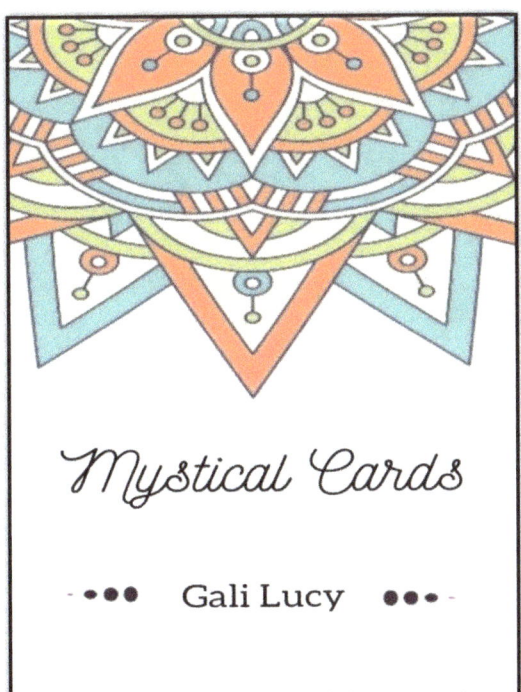

Mystical Cards

· •●● Gali Lucy ●●• ·

16

Writing

A new path opens to you.
Writing will help you
unleash emotions, share and
heal your soul.
Nothing is yours - everything
already exists and is delivered
to you from heaven. You are a
spirit within a temporary
material body, an important
link in a long chain.
Gates open and knowledge
will flow to you, remove ego
and listen to criticism.
Generosity produces
looping abundance.

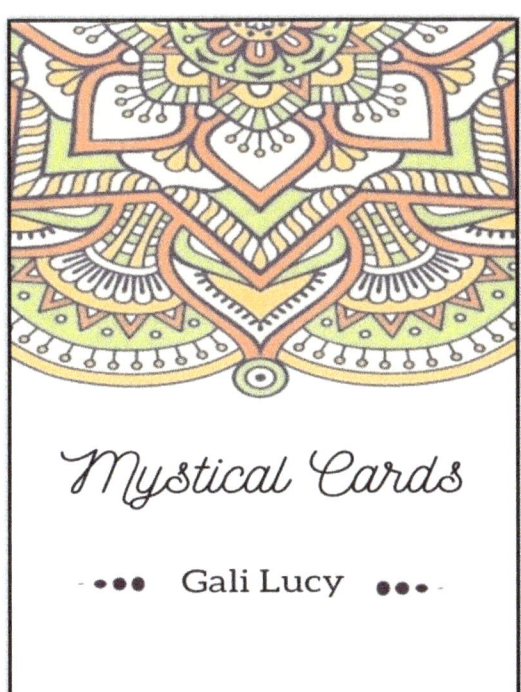

Mystical Cards

••• Gali Lucy •••

17

Perfection

A tendency toward **perfection**
creates a sense of frustration,
guilt, and a desire to correct
the soul through matter.
Nothing is accidental
or self-evident, learn to
appreciate what you have.
All that is created is valuable
and perfect, don't copy be
original. You have a lot
to give to others, trust and
connect to the right people.
Initiative will bring you
abundance.

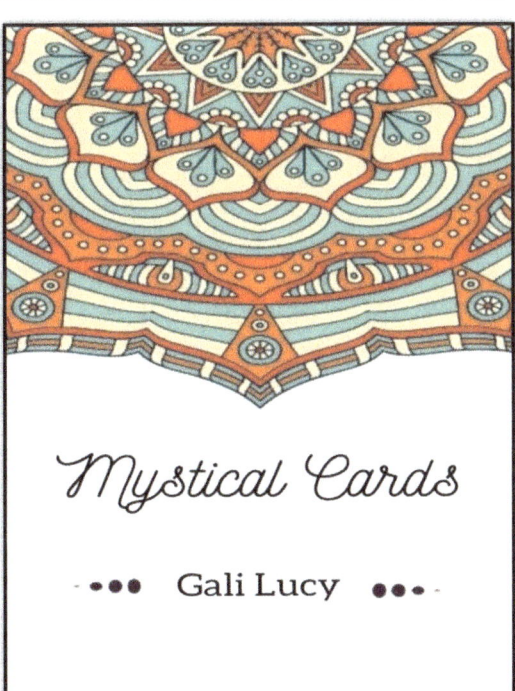

Mystical Cards

··••• Gali Lucy •••··

18

Openness

Act with **openness** to cultures, languages and opinions, and share feelings. Be humble, disconnect from disruption and connect with new pleasures. Learn to forgive and respect the choice of others. Any problem will be resolved if you understand its source and reason. Communication will bring ideas and collaborations. Spirituality will heal and improve your life and health.

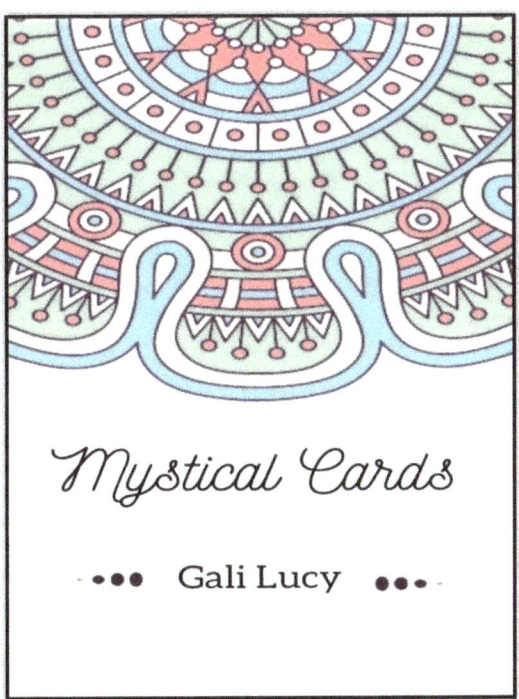

𝓜ystical 𝓒ards

••• Gali Lucy •••

19

Satisfaction

You are heading for a period
of **satisfaction**, promotion
and success. Every difficulty
in your life has been
summoned on you and every
failure is meant to empower
you. Focus on the doing
and make connections.
Turn ideas into new projects.
Communication, initiative,
perseverance and giving
are your tools. The Creation
will give you what you
need and not what you want.
Smile to life.

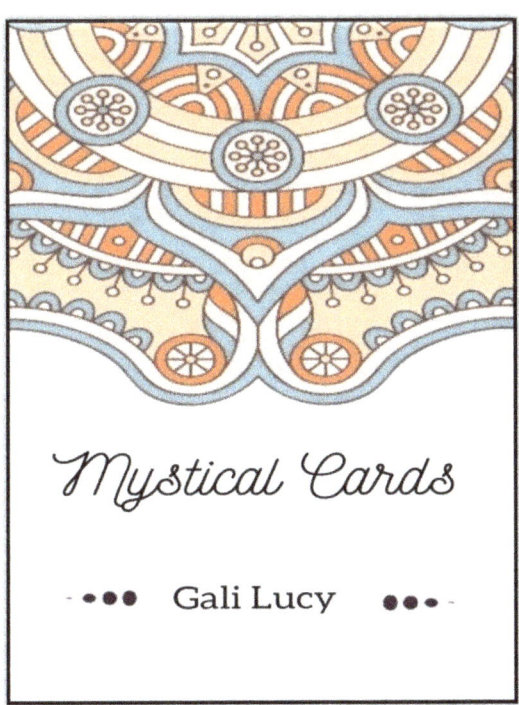

Mystical Cards

•• Gali Lucy ••

20

Work

There is a desire for a change
in **work**. Check if the timing
is correct. Work wisely and
patiently and remember that
every difficulty is
summoned by you.
Avoid jealousy, criticism
and stubbornness.
Listen to your intuition,
share your thoughts
with superiors and plan wisely.
Your actions will reward
you with abundance,
health, happiness,
satisfaction, and success.

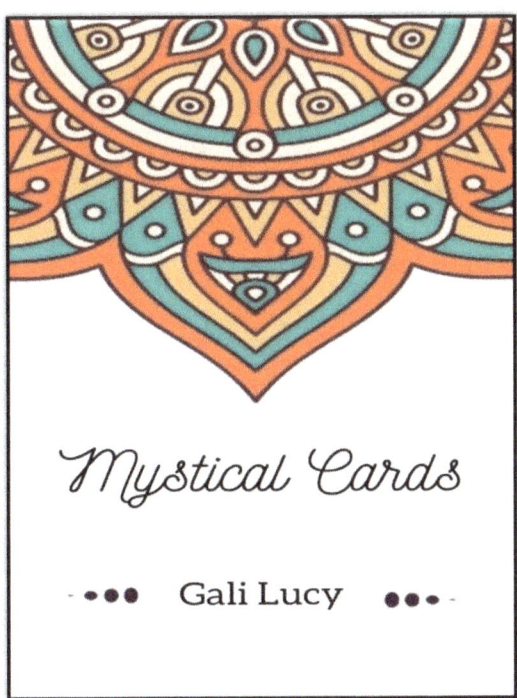

Mystical Cards

· •●● Gali Lucy ●●• ·

21

Hope

There are no coincidences,
all has been created for you.
Do not lose **hope** because you
do not yet understand your
destiny and lesson. Courage
and faith are required,
messages are sent to you
in dreams and through
people and use humor and
creativity. Finish repairing
with people from the past,
which will help you relax.
You are heading for a time of
satisfaction, pleasure
and new friendships.

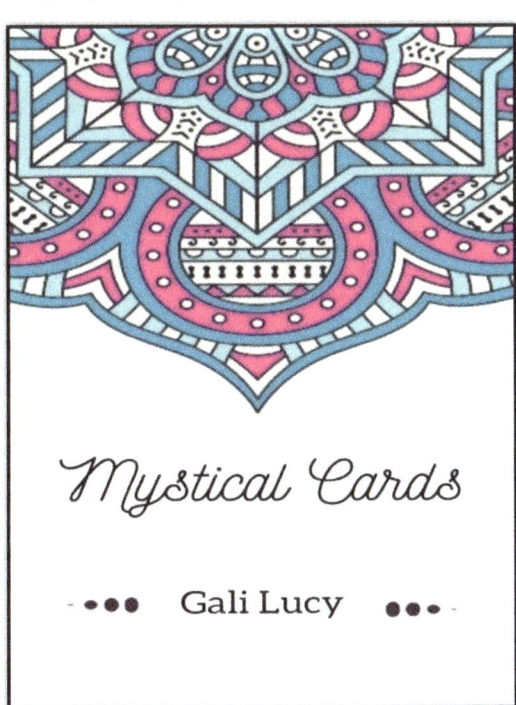

Mystical Cards

- •• Gali Lucy ••• -

22

Willpower

You are in a test period and you will require **willpower**, perseverance, and a positive attitude. You can change the life script and write yourself a new destiny. There are no penalties but life lessons. With patience and courage you will be opened to new communities and projects. It's a time for forgiveness and trust.
You are preparing for a renewed acceleration which will bring to light your fruits.

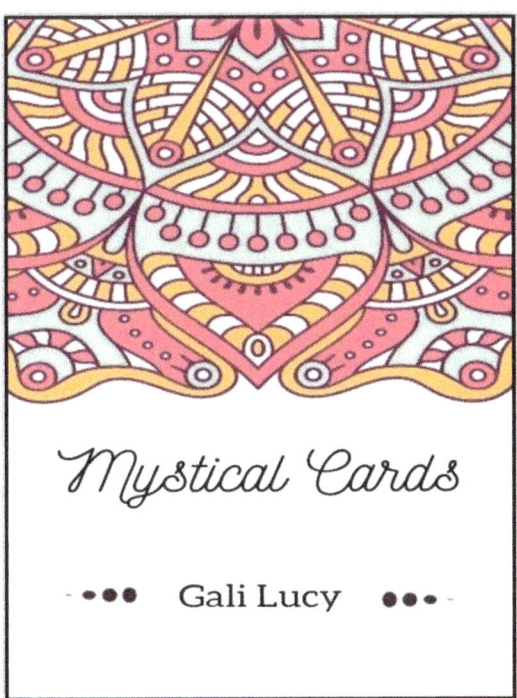

Mystical Cards

- ••• Gali Lucy ••• -

23

Interruptions

The current situation cannot
be quite seen due to
interruptions.
Close-mindedness,
stubbornness, self-pity,
and criticism caused
frustration and loneliness.
Jealousy and comparison
are unnecessary.
You are heading for
a makeover in your
life if you will listen to
others and act with ego-less
wisdom. You are
protected from heaven.

Mystical Cards

•●● Gali Lucy ●●•

24

Growth

You are heading for
a turnaround and **growth**.
After a long period of
stuckness, suggestions and
knowledge will soon appear
to give you happiness
and improvement. Accept the
past as a lesson for the best.
Intuition and life wisdom will
help you understand what you
need to change. You were
born to complete your karma
and experience feelings as a
spirit within a material body.
Your wisdom will help others.

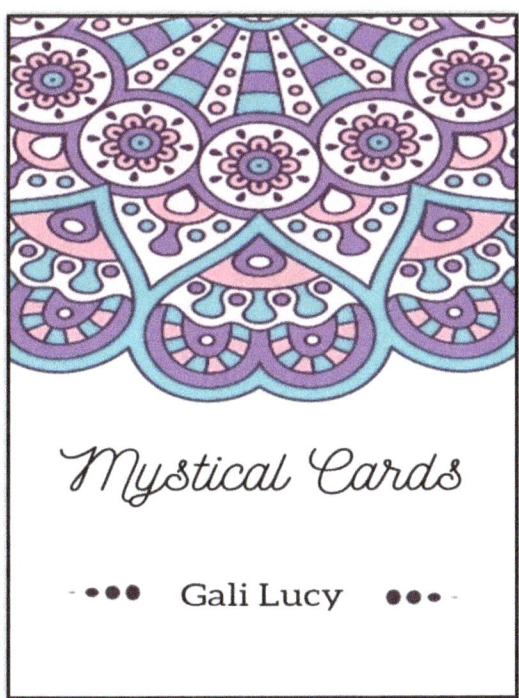

Mystical Cards

••• Gali Lucy •••

25

Powerful

There is inner **powerful**
strength and wisdom
in you which will lead
to learning and collaboration
worldwide. Nothing restricts
you, make order and
remove the unnecessary.
A short noisy period and
struggles are expected
to pave your way.
Get help from friends,
learn to respect the
choice of others
as part of your closure.

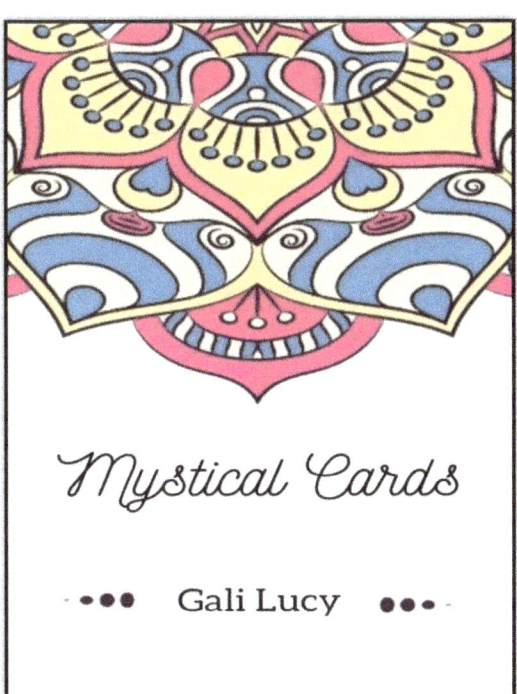

Mystical Cards

• • • Gali Lucy • • •

26

Balance

Balance in life comes
through the right
combination of mind and
emotion. Wisdom and mutual
respect will help you
realize your goals,
agreements and connections.
Avoid stress and guilt.
Forgive the past and
enjoy the present, it's time to
fulfill dreams. Open up to
cultures, languages and travel.
Wisdom is within the quiet
person, meditation
will get you there.

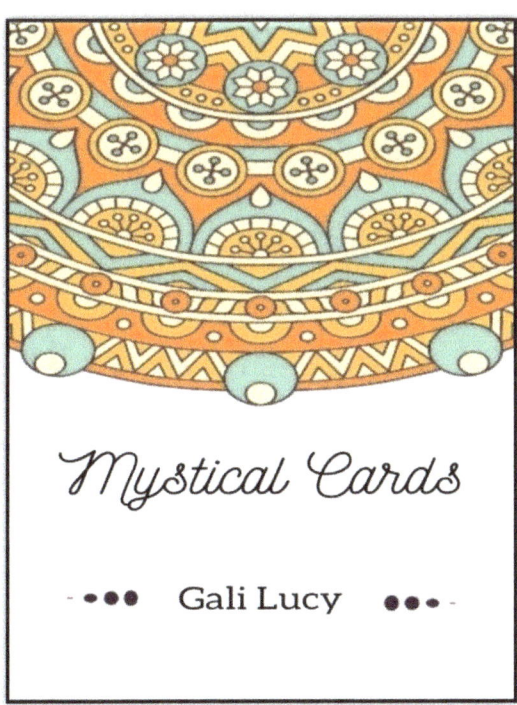

Mystical Cards

•• Gali Lucy ••

27

Energy

Anger, frustration and
disappointment create
distrust and remoteness.
Negative thoughts consume
energy and time. Your thoughts
have the power to create
the reality of your life.
Remember that you have
chosen everything to experience.
You are heading for a time
full of abundance, opportunity,
reward, and satisfaction from
whatever you planted.
Let Creation surprise
you for the best.

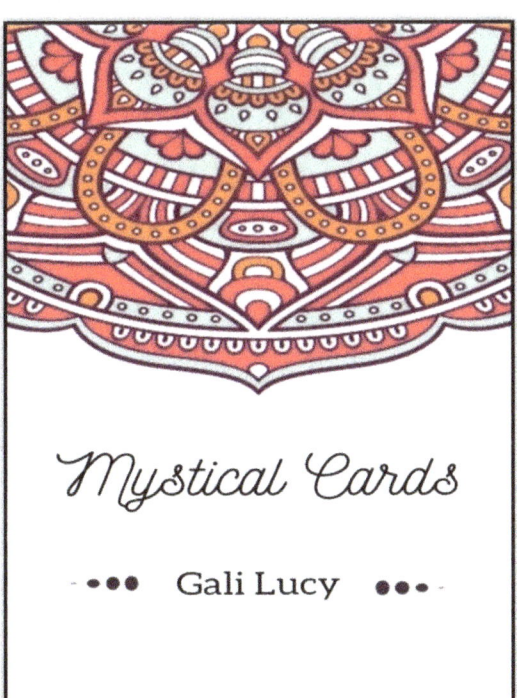

Mystical Cards

••• Gali Lucy •••

28

Letting Go

Letting go of ego and
stubbornness is the way to
empowerment. Avoid
negative thoughts, criticisms
and quick conclusions.
Everything that has happened
in your life is for your benefit.
The Creation gives you
obstacles so you can
overcome and mature. Life
lessons are an asset and not
a punishment. It is advisable
to end burdensome
relationships in order
to allow abundance to enter.

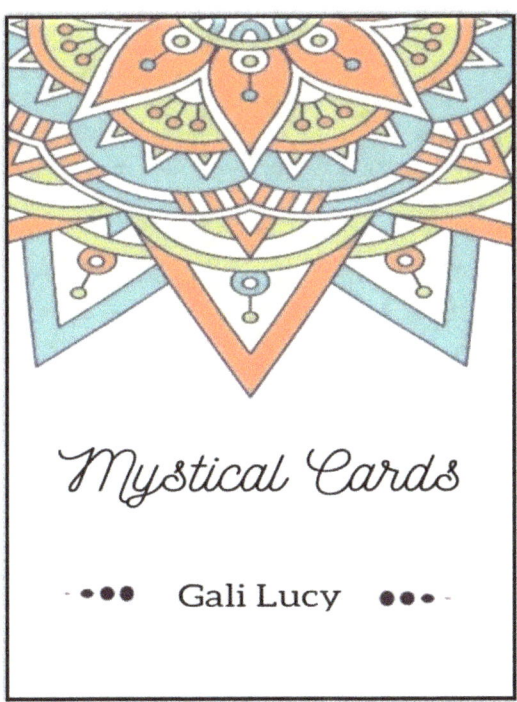

Mystical Cards

··•• Gali Lucy ••·

29

Planning

Any **planning** in your life is
unnecessary, let The Creation
lead you, release control
and listen to your intuition.
There is no coincidence,
everything goes wrong for
the best. Every mistake is
a new start. Get support from
spiritualists and friends for
new knowledge and insights.
Studying and engaging in
a variety of fields will allow
you to use your abilities.
Social networks will
enrich your life.

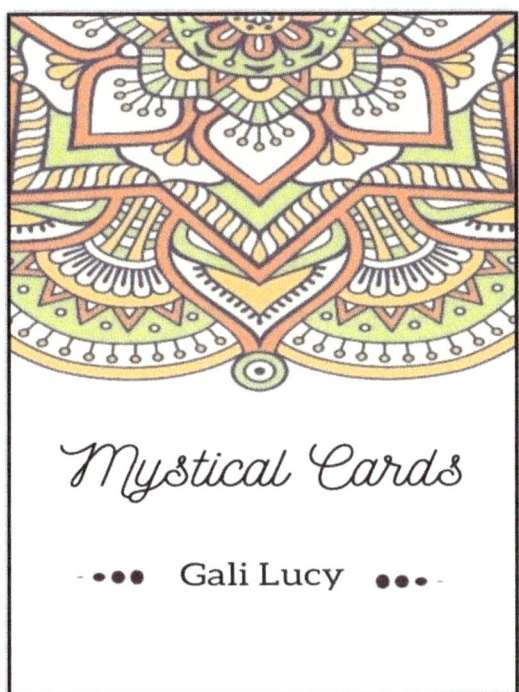

Mystical Cards

·••• Gali Lucy •••·

30

Wisdom

The source of **wisdom** lies
in the childhood and reincarnation
of the soul, where fears and pains
also exist. Difficulty is designed to
strengthen and end your karma.
Through who you are not - you will
understand who you are.
A character will come into your life
and wake you up. Goals will be
achieved with patience and
wisdom. The Creation narrows
your options to make you
understand and complete what is
missing. You are in the process of
changing directions for the best.

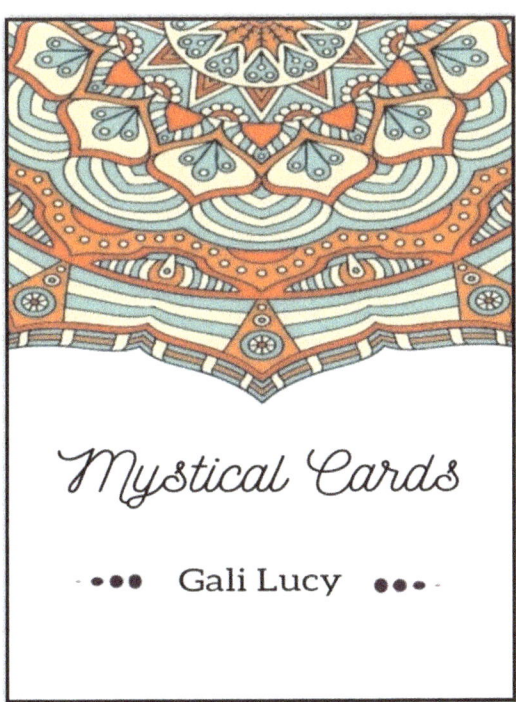

Mystical Cards

· ••• Gali Lucy ••• ·

31

Courage

You have the **courage** to
resist compromises, it's
time to demand what you
deserve. Avoid frustration
and fear of change.
Learn to flex and listen
to your inner voice.
You are protected and
the road is wide open to you.
Pave new bridges, success
and change are ahead of
you. Do not wait to be
rescued, only you will save
yourself. Knowledge is the
main tool for personal
development and abundance.

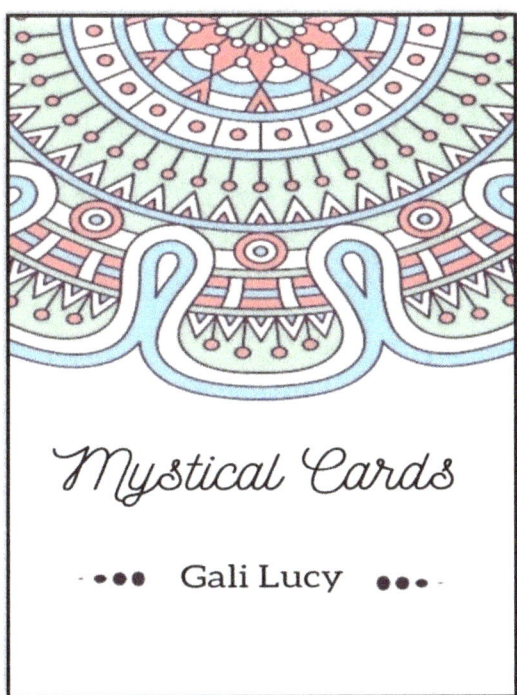

Mystical Cards

··· Gali Lucy ···

32

Art

Know to bring feelings and
emotions through **art**,
writing, dancing,
and music. A new
project will make
you happy. Clear anger,
leave the past behind you,
the future is navigated
by you. Connect with
people worldwide.
Live like it's your
last day, adopt a healthy
lifestyle and travel.
Opportunities are
open to you.

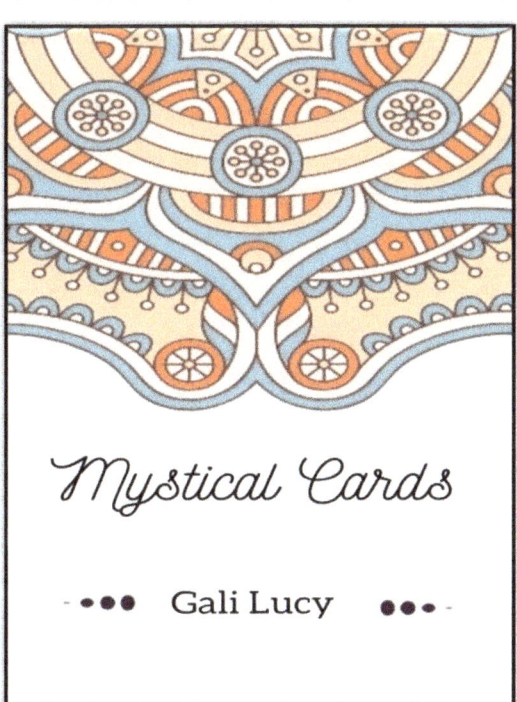

Mystical Cards

- •●● Gali Lucy ●●• -

33

Relationship

Relationship and caring
is the main thing.
There is a fear of
abandonment and failure.
Place the past behind you
and avoid criticism and
judgment, create yourself
opportunities and new
relationships, social
media will help you
reach the goal.
Look for the one who will
complete you.
Say: "I'm about to have"
instead of: "I don't have."

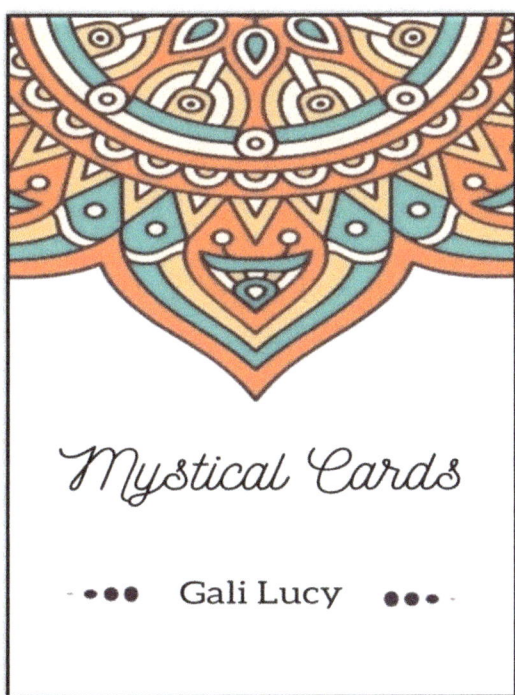

Mystical Cards

···•• Gali Lucy ••·

34

Contact

Get yourself engaged in
new healing, **contact**, and
relationships. Upgrade
communication skills
and external appearance.
Learn to initiate and accept,
emerge out of loneliness,
stubbornness, criticism
and judgment. Avoid
jumping to conclusions.
Exercising and traveling
will have a positive impact.
Treat yourself to spa
treatments, happiness
is in the small pleasures.

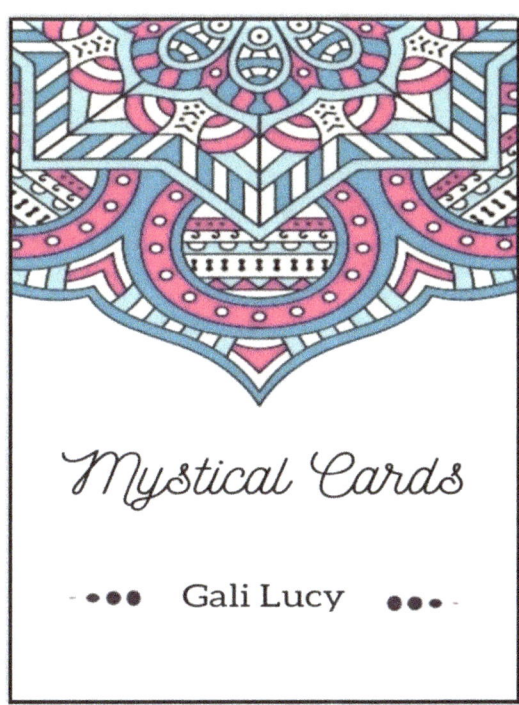

Mystical Cards

- •●● Gali Lucy ●●• -

35

Insight

Insight, knowledge and
wisdom come through
failures and life experience.
You have the power to strengthen
or crush others and yourself.
Try to understand that everything
is brought to
you for your own good.
Switch war with listening
and love. All that is given to you
should not be taken
for granted, learn to take
advantage of every moment
as it will pass. Things will begin
to work in your favor,
listen to your spiritual guidance.

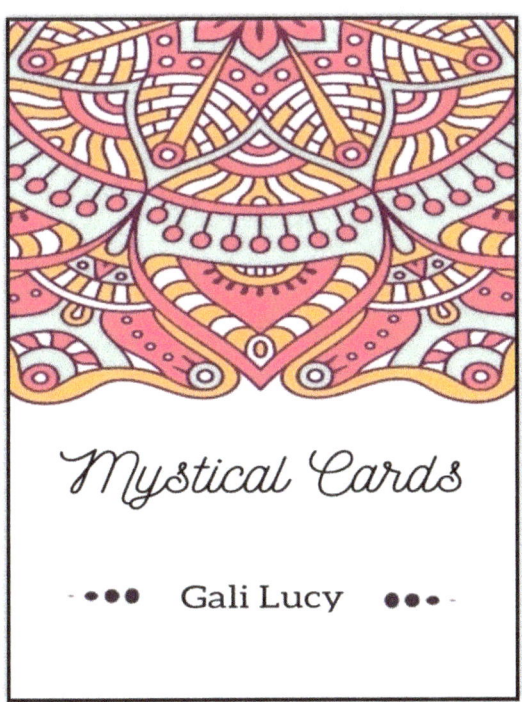

Mystical Cards

- •• **Gali Lucy** ••• -

36

Initiative

Achieving success in life
does not depend only on you,
but on others. **Initiative,**
communication and
mutual support will give
you success, abundance,
friendships and new
positions. You are not
a victim, avoid stubbornness.
Be wise and less right.
You will give your
knowledge to others who
will reward
you in the future, healing is
on the way to you.

Mystical Cards

••• Gali Lucy •••

37

Beginning

A **beginning** of a new journey
is ahead of you,
gifts and abundance will flow
to you. Friendships, travel,
change of location, or making
agreements are expected.
Each end is a means for
a new beginning. Flow
and don't dismiss moves
from fear and vulnerability
from your past. Social media
and collaborations will
help you achieve your goals.
Cast your bread upon
the water, which will
return to you.

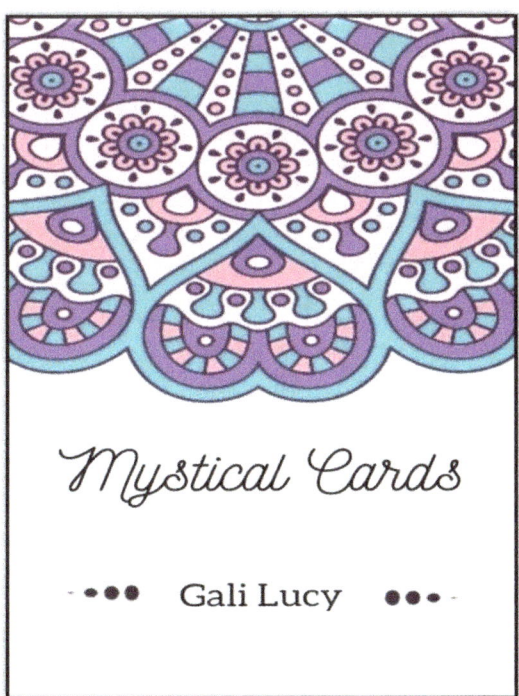

Mystical Cards

• • • Gali Lucy • • •

38

Secure

After a long period of time,
things start to work out.
You will begin to feel
secure financially,
family and health wise.
Changes, transitions,
and travels will enrich
you with knowledge
and enjoyment.
Rise over difficulties
which will gradually
disappear on the way
to resolution.
Take away fears and
let intuition lead you.

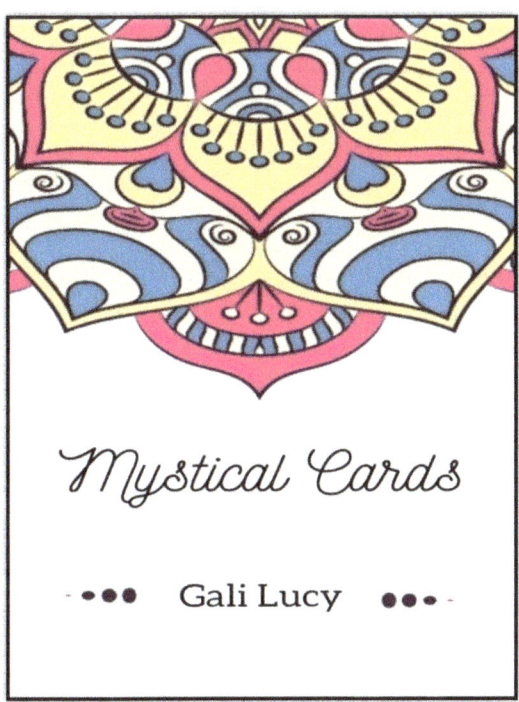

Mystical Cards

· •• Gali Lucy •• ·

39

Goal

Don't compromise, set
yourself one **goal** at a time.
Learn from mistakes and
allow yourself to make
mistakes. Be original,
no need to resemble others,
you are as wonderful as you
are. Physical state reflects
a state of mind, it's time to
disengage from anything
that gets in your way.
All your actions come back
to you, so do good
without hurting others.
Opportunities are
open to you.

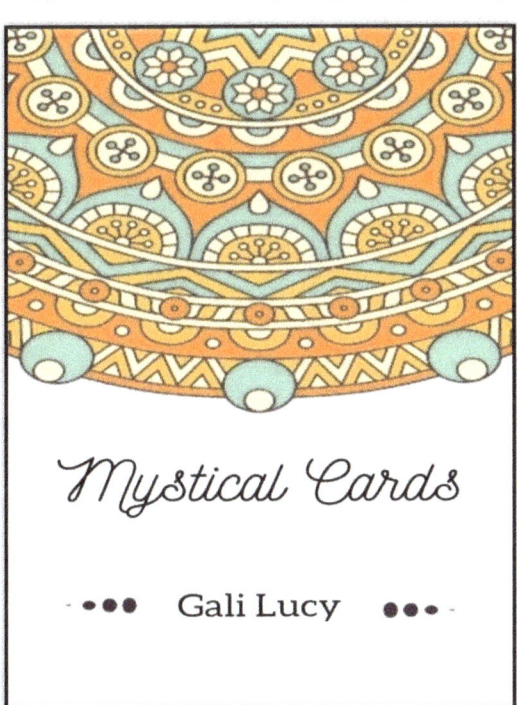

Mystical Cards

••• Gali Lucy •••

40

Healing

Now is the time for **healing**
your mind and body,
every illness stems from
lack of forgiveness and fear.
You have chosen the script
of your life in advance
and life lessons are not
punishable, so remove
self-pity. Trust and approach
people. Your life is about to
change, being collaborative
will provide you with
insight, peace, knowledge,
and success.
Use alternative healing.

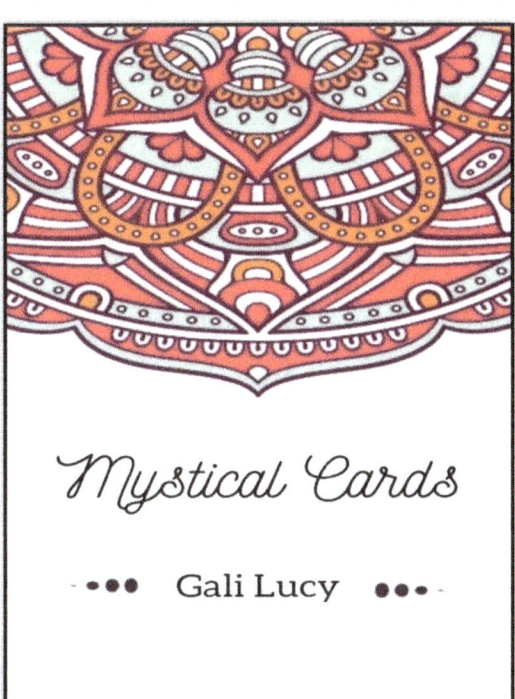

Mystical Cards

••• Gali Lucy •••

41

Knowledge

Knowledge is power,
use it wisely, criticism
and frustration prevent you
from reaching abundance
and rest. Every beginning
requires chaos. Every day
is a new opportunity.
Share the knowledge
you have gathered so
that you will have success
and recognition. Don't
be angry at your past,
enjoy every moment as
it passes. Everything went
wrong for the best.

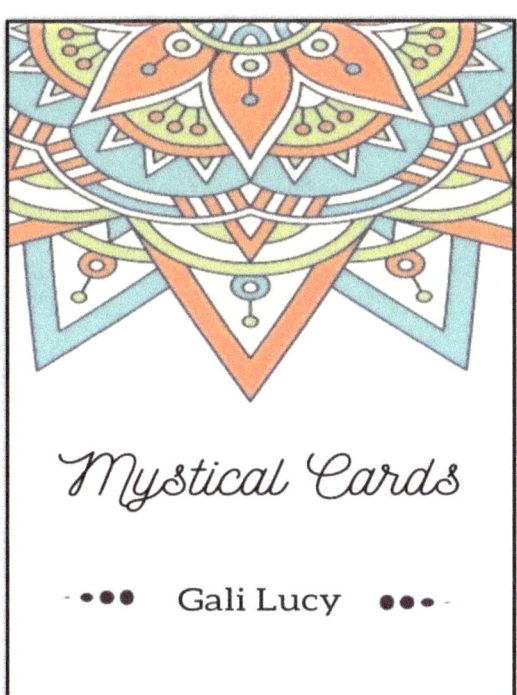

Mystical Cards

• •• Gali Lucy ••• •

42

Health

Take care of your health.
Set down your war tools
aside and turn to your heart,
wisdom, and compassion.
Every illness comes from
your previous life,
unconscious fear, anger,
tenacity, and self-pity.
The physical body is
the mirror of the soul.
Difficulty from the past
will disappear if you'll
let it go and use healing
methods and your
health will gradually improve.

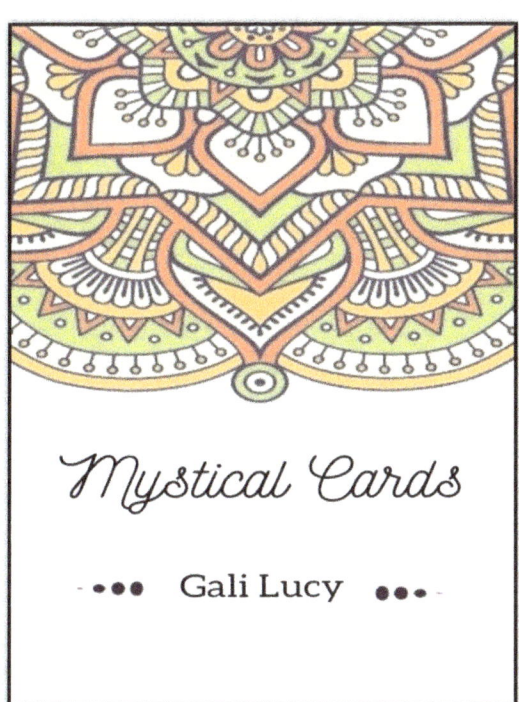

Mystical Cards

••• Gali Lucy •••

43

Happiness

Every door that closes
opens others.
Follow your happiness and
the universe will open up
doors for you where there
were only walls before.
Happiness lies in the little things.
Reorganize your life in order
and avoid dependency.
Open your heart to opportunities,
learn to approach others through
humor and optimism.
New relationships are
at your doorway.

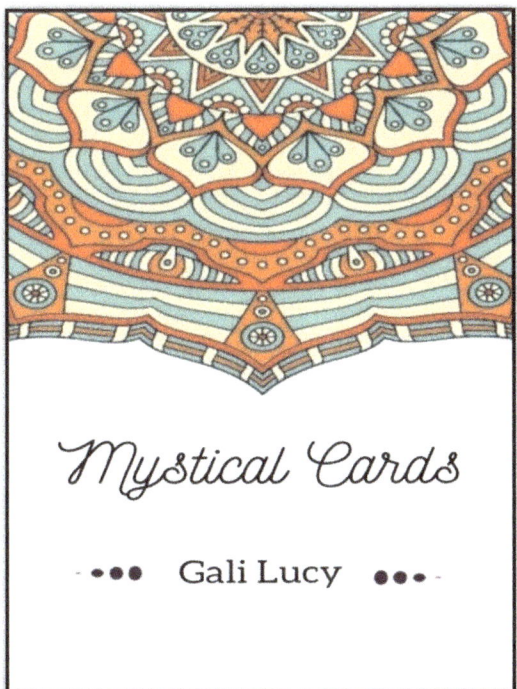

Mystical Cards

· ••• Gali Lucy •••·

44

Communication

You have the power to
change your life and
health for the better.
The body and mind are one.
Don't look for justice, use
communication wisely.
Ask for good things to
come to you. Push aside
everything that ended
its role in your life.
Abundance will come,
spend it wisely.
Adopt a healthy and
relaxing lifestyle. Be open to
social media and new friendships.

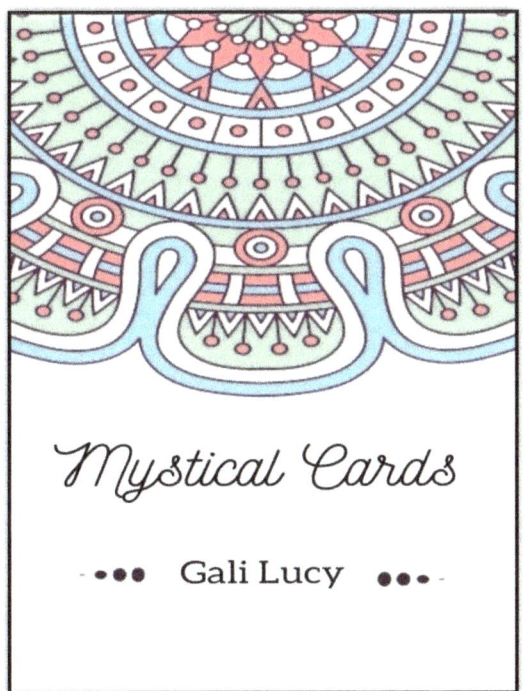

Mystical Cards

••• Gali Lucy •••

45

Opportunity

A new opportunity will
come in and improve
your quality of life.
The Creation closes doors for
you, in order for you to
open other doors elsewhere.
Get rid of dependency and
criticism, everything is for
your own good.
Difficulties will gradually
fade away and good news
are on the way.
It's a good time to study,
humor and collaborations
will promote you.

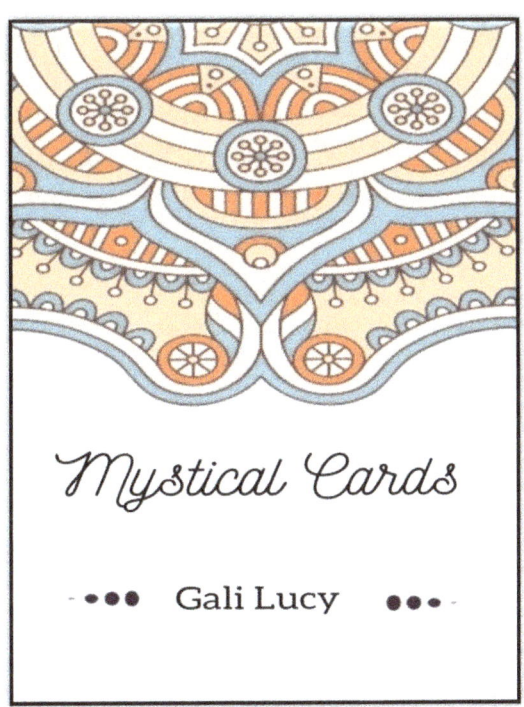

Mystical Cards

· ●●● Gali Lucy ●●● ·

46

Understanding

Your soul does not
know how to relax.
An understanding of
past mistakes is needed.
Anger and frustration
come from inappropriate
choices you have made.
New opportunities are at
the doorway. Avoid judging
changes in advance.
Positive thinking and
perseverance are required.
Suggestions will come and will
change a fixed mindset on the
road to success.

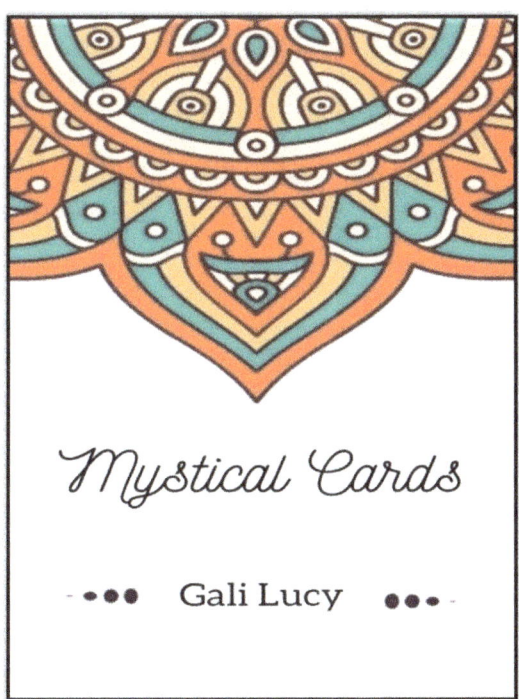

Mystical Cards

•• Gali Lucy ••

47

Learning

Learning, investing and
perseverance are necessary
to achieve goals. Listen to your
intuition and choose a path.
More opportunities will
come later, free yourself from
stubbornness and have more
patience. Organize and arrange
your thinking. The great inventions
were created
as a result of mistakes.
Reward and success will
come if you know how to
enjoy it. New friendships will
give you happiness and help.

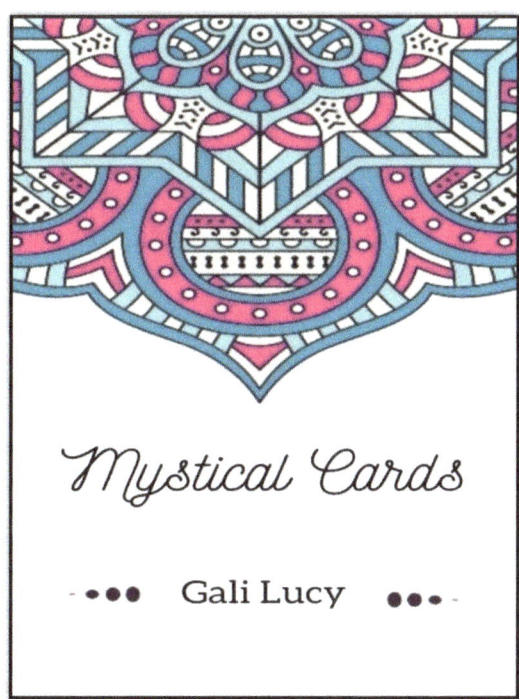

Mystical Cards

· •●● Gali Lucy ●●• ·

48

Quiet

This is a difficult period
for you with restlessness.
It looks like you've
reached a dead end and
you need quiet, calmness
and balance.
Get away from anything
that gets in your way.
Exercise wisdom and intuition,
remove the unnecessary.
Open up to people,
nature, animals, music,
and everything that gives
you happiness.
Find help in spirituality.

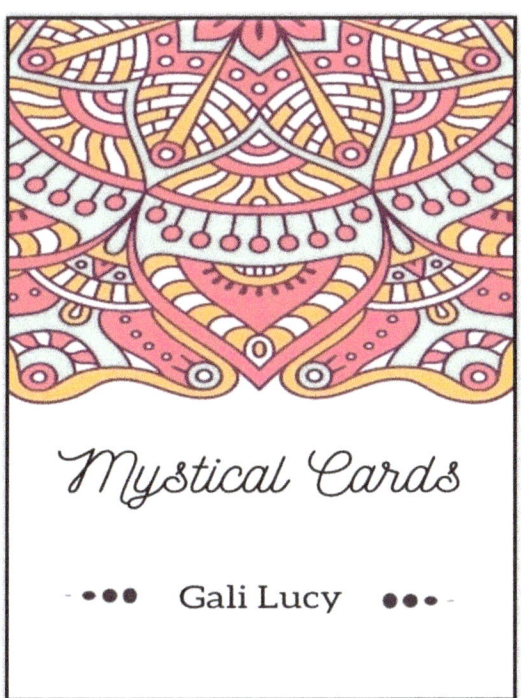

Mystical Cards

••• Gali Lucy •••

49

Giving

Be giving to others
without expecting to
receive back. Give first
to yourself and then to
others in order to not
get drained.
We are all guests
here for a moment.
Communicating and helping
the community will
provide you success
and collaboration,
in this way you create
endless reciprocity.
You are protected and guarded.

Mystical Cards

· •●● Gali Lucy ●●• ·

49

50

Respect

You can't buy respect,
because it's gained through
giving and listening to others.
Master how to take advantage
of the present for your future and
not get stuck in the past. Learn to
free yourself with
love and less anger.
Take responsibility and don't
blame others for your mistakes.
The words that come out of your
mouth have the power to create
or destroy. All your actions
come back to you in your
lifetime. Success and luck
will open up to you.

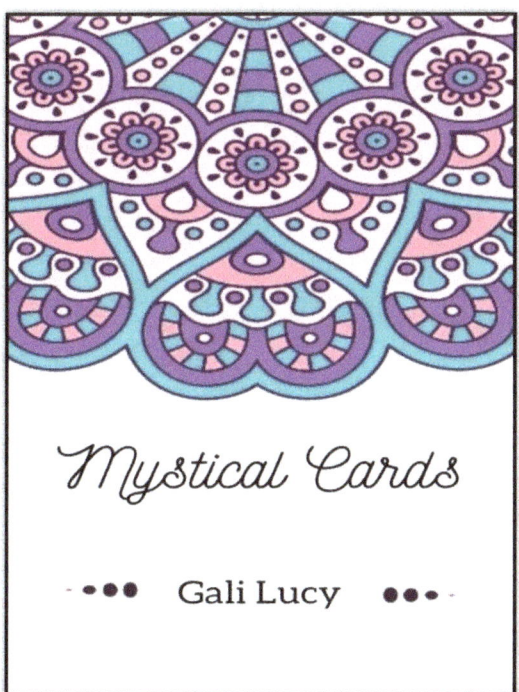

Mystical Cards

•●● Gali Lucy ●●•

51

Caring

Caring is the universal
frequency required
for all souls. You are
about to have
new friendships
and partnerships.
Avoid criticism
and judgment.
Social media exposure
will help to expose you.
Look for the one who
will complete you.
Enjoy the journey
of your life.

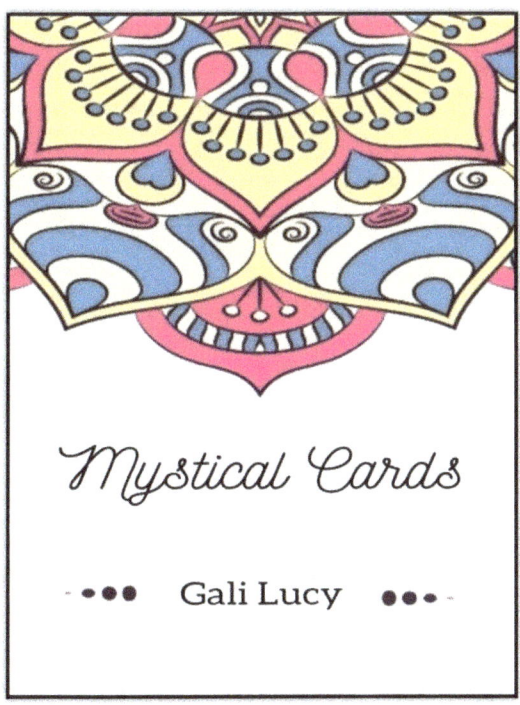

Mystical Cards

• • • Gali Lucy • • •

52

Creation

You are a spirit in
a temporary human body,
which is an important link in
the process of Creation.
Remember it's not
possible to die, but only to
move between spirit and matter.
Your soul is endless and
chooses to dwell in a living
body for a limited time,
to correct and complete
lessons from your past life.
You can only experience
feelings in a human body.
You are ahead of new
insight and success.

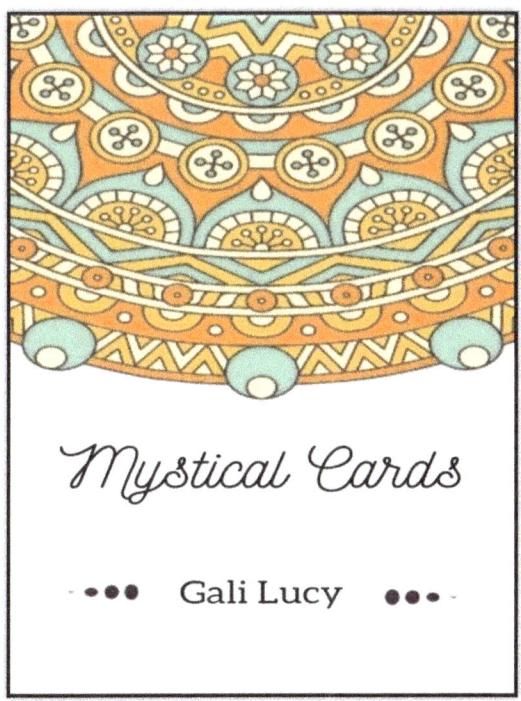

Mystical Cards

· •●● Gali Lucy ●●• ·

Summary words

Dear readers,

I hope you enjoyed my book. Accept the insights of the book as additional opinions, because there will never be a single truth, in order to allow you a free choice.
The circle of life, has no beginning and no end, nothing can be destroyed, everything is an infinite circle. Therefore, it is impossible to die, you are infinite balls of lights, who choose to reside in a human body on Earth, in order to testify of your nature and thus, to testify to the nature of God.

For further reading, you are welcome to read my four other books, which were also channeled through me by *The Creation Entities,* and I typed them directly into the computer:

1. Divine Creation:
offers the readers with the meaning of life, who is God / *The Creation, The Creators,* and *The Created.* Who created humanity on Earth? What is the purpose of humanity? and many other topics and insights.

2. The Aquarius Age:
offers the readers with information as humanity is separating from the Pisces Age and entering the

incoming Aquarius Age, which is affected by the Zodiac's movement on Earth. The signs of this new age: revealing the truth, fast justice, power returning to the masses, replacing governments with communities, revolutions led mostly by women, and creating heaven on Earth.

3. The Future: Based on the Ages theory

provides the readers with astrological and numerological research and information regarding how the Zodiac aligns with the pages of history. In this research, I moved in time 4,000 years backwards and 25,000 years forward, and discovered there is a mathematical pattern, which has allowed humanity to understand what happened in the past and predict the future, according to the Zodiac movement.

4. Lenormand Tarot Deck Meaning: A guidebook channeled through Anne-Marie Adelaide's spirit

Madame Lenormand was a psychic for over 40 years and gained much publicity and recognition in Europe for the advice she gave to Napoleon and his wife Josephine, the leaders of the French Revolution, and the French aristocrats. Upon her retirement from work, she returned to her hometown as a wealthy woman, even wealthier than the king of France. After her death, she didn't leave behind detailed information on how to read her cards.

Hence, in 2014 Gali Lucy decided to contact her, and received simple instructions regarding how to read them. She wrote this guidebook for half a year thanks to Madame Lenormand's permission to channel with her.

You are balls of lights embodied in a temporary material body as a soul, while your actions testify to the nature of God.

You are welcome to listen to my frequency singing, while *The Creation Entities* also channeled through me, as it reaches, relaxes, and heals the soul, on my **YouTube Channel** and website www.Gali4u.com.

Book a telephone channeling session from my website.

About the author

Gali Lucy

Medium, Author, Singer, Composer, and Architecture

Engineer, who channels with *The Creation's Entities* since the age of six.

She channels through her brain without any additional tools and advises on a variety of topics world-wide.

She gained vast experience and positive reputation for accuracy in predicting the future, both on a personal and global level, using X-ray remote vision ability.

She is the author of the following spiritual books:
1. Divine Creation
2. The Future: Based on the Ages theory
3. The Aquarius Age
4. Messages from the Mystical Cards
5. Lenormand Tarot Deck Meaning: A guidebook channeled through Anne-Marie Adelaide's spirit

These books were dictated to her through channeling with an easy and simple explanation and information, regarding what is *The Creation's* plan for humanity on planet Earth and to prepare mankind into the entrance of the Aquarius Age.

She also sings frequency songs without background music in her **Gali Lucy YouTube Channel**, while *The Creation's Entities* are channeling through her.

Author Website: www.Gali4u.com

www.ingramcontent.com/pod-product-compliance
Lightning Source LLC
Chambersburg PA
CBHW071202120626
46546CB00006B/2384